Biomes
of North
America

A Journey into an Estuary

by Rebecca L. Johnson

with illustrations by Phyllis V. Saroff

CAROLRHODA BOOKS, INC./MINNEAPOLIS

Carolrhoda Books, Inc.
A division of Lerner Publishing Group
241 First Avenue North
Minneapolis, Minnesota 55401 U.S.A.

Website address: www.lernerbooks.com

Library of Congress Cataloging-in-Publication Data

Johnson, Rebecca L.
    A journey into an estuary / by Rebecca L. Johnson ; with
illustrations by Phyllis V. Saroff.
      p.   cm. — (Biomes of North America)
    Summary: Takes readers on a walk at a sheltered bay, showing
examples of how the animals and plants of estuaries are connected
and dependent on each other and the estuary's mix of fresh and
salt water.
    ISBN: 1-57505-592-9 (lib. bdg. : alk. paper)
    1. Estuarine ecology—Juvenile literature. 2. Estuaries—Juvenile
literature. [1. Estuarine ecology. 2. Estuaries. 3. Ecology.] I.
Saroff, Phyllis L., ill. II. Title. III. Series.
QH541.5.E8J64 2004
577.7'86—dc22   2003015090

Manufactured in the United States of America
1 2 3 4 5 6 – JR – 09 08 07 06 05 04

Words to Know

ALGAE (AL-jee)—plantlike living things that use sunlight to make their own food

BRACKISH (BRA-kish)—water that is a mixture of saltwater and freshwater

ESTUARY (EHS-choo-air-ee)—the water biome formed where a river meets the ocean

FOOD CHAIN—the connection among living things that shows what eats what in an ecosystem

MARSH—a wetland where most of the plants are grasses

MUDFLAT—a muddy area that is covered by water at high tide

PLANKTON (PLANK-tuhn)—a collection of tiny organisms that drifts through the estuary water. Plankton is eaten by many estuary animals.

PREDATOR (PREH-duh-tur)—an animal that hunts and eats other animals

PREY (PRAY)—an animal that is hunted and eaten by other animals

TIDE—the daily movement of the entire ocean slowly toward the land or away from it

WATER BIOME (BYE-ohm)—a major community of living things in a water-based area, such as a lake or river

WETLAND—an area of land that is covered by shallow water all or part of the year

Ripples
on calm water

A great blue heron strides on long legs through the shallow water. She scans the surface, watching and waiting. A small ripple catches her eye. The heron freezes, still as a statue.

Suddenly, she stabs down with her spearlike beak and comes up with a squirming silver fish. Spreading her wings, the heron flies off across the estuary to a nest where her hungry chicks are waiting.

An estuary is a place where a river meets the ocean. It is a kingdom of brown and green and blue, part wet and part dry. In an estuary, fresh river water and salty ocean water mix to form a special environment that brims with life.

Estuaries are found along the edges of continents and islands. Some are broad and shallow. Others are narrow and deep. There are estuaries that stretch far inland and estuaries that hug the coast.

Estuaries form where waves of salty ocean water wash inland and mix with freshwater flowing from a river.

Sunlight sparkles on shallow water at an estuary's ocean edge (above) *and farther inland* (left)*, where grasses and distant trees grow.*

7

In and around a river (right), plants and animals are adapted to life in fast-moving freshwater. Those that live in the ocean (below) are adapted to a saltwater home.

Estuaries are one kind of the earth's bodies of water. The largest of these is the salty ocean. The ocean covers nearly 75 percent of the earth's surface. Smaller bodies of water include freshwater lakes, rivers, and wetlands.

Together lakes, rivers, wetlands, estuaries, and the ocean make up the earth's water biomes. A water biome is a water-based region that is home to a unique group of living things. These living things are all adapted, or specially suited, to living in that region.

Each biome's living things, from tiny microscopic creatures to large plants and animals, form a community. Each member of that community depends on the others. All these living things, in turn, depend on the water—fresh or salty, moving or still—that forms their watery home. They swim through it, find food in it, and are carried from place to place by it. Without the water, they could not survive.

The still waters of a shallow lake are a source of food for a great egret.

The water in an estuary is a mixture of freshwater and saltwater. This mix is called brackish water. The closer you are to the ocean, the saltier the water is.

The amount of saltwater in an estuary also depends on the ocean tides. Twice a day, the edge of the ocean slowly comes up higher on the shore. Then it gradually moves back out toward the horizon. The "coming in" and "going out" of the water is called a tide. When the water comes in, it's high tide. When the water goes out, it's low tide.

At high tide (above), ocean water moves up into an estuary. At low tide (left), the water pulls back, exposing some of the land.

Exposed at low tide, a half-buried clam closes its shell with a snap—and squirts water high in the air.

When the tide is high, saltwater from the ocean flows into an estuary, making the water saltier. When the tide is low, ocean water moves out of the estuary, and the water in the estuary becomes less salty. The plants and animals that live in estuaries must survive these constantly changing conditions. What is salty one hour may be fresh the next. What is underwater in the morning may be out of the water at noon.

The great blue heron lives in a large estuary. There she is again, soaring high overhead. The heron is looking for more food. Let's follow her on a journey into the estuary.

The heron peers across the mudflat at low tide. At high tide, the mudflat is covered by ocean water.

The heron flies to the outer edge of the estuary, close to the ocean. She circles once, then lands on a long, flat stretch of mud.

It's damp and breezy on the mudflat. The sharp tang of salt fills the air. From off in the distance comes the rhythmic *whoosh, whoosh, whoosh* of ocean waves hitting the shore.

Where does all this mud come from? The river water that flows into the estuary is full of tiny particles of dirt and sand. As the water moves slowly toward the ocean, these particles sink to the bottom and form a deep layer of soft mud.

The mud is full of nutrients that living things need to live and grow. Some nutrients come from the river water that enters the estuary. Other nutrients wash in from the ocean with the tides.

Much of the mud in an estuary comes from dirt carried downstream in river water.

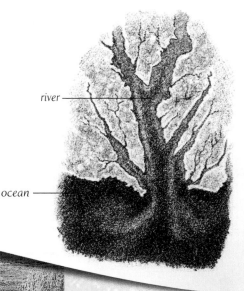

river

ocean

The mudflat looks empty compared to parts of the estuary where plants grow. But the mud is packed with nutrients—and life.

13

Tube worms and clams live just under the mud's surface, where they are well hidden from predators.

Razor clams get their name from the sharp edges on their shells.

The heron walks slowly along, leaving a trail of footprints. She pokes her long bill into the soft mud, searching for food. Hiding just beneath the surface are many-legged bristle worms, paper-thin ribbon worms, and tiny tube worms. Venus clams and razor clams share the mud with the worms.

Clams use a muscular foot to dig through the mud. When the tide is high, they suck in water through tubes that stick up above the mud like miniature snorkels.

Dozens of mud snails creep slowly over the mudflat. They graze on seaweed that lies limp in the hot sun. A slimy coating prevents the seaweed from drying out until the ocean water returns.

A clam draws water into its body through a tubelike siphon, filters out food particles, and pumps the filtered water out through a second siphon.

A mud snail bulldozes a path through the mud.

Only male fiddler crabs have a huge front claw, which they use to scare off other males and impress females.

The heron spots a bold fiddler crab that scuttles past on spindly legs. The crab waves its one big claw back and forth, like a fist. The heron takes a step closer. But before she can strike, the fiddler crab dives into the safety of its underground burrow.

Moments later, a smaller fiddler crab is not so lucky. The heron grabs it with her bill and swallows it whole.

At low tide, fiddler crabs roam the mudflat, nibbling on seaweed and the remains of dead estuary creatures.

An oystercatcher's long, sturdy beak is the perfect tool for breaking open oyster and clam shells.

Low tide on the mudflat means a feast for other birds too. Wilson's plovers prance across the mudflats, plucking crabs from their hiding places. Spotted sandpipers peck rapidly at the mud. They snap up worms and other tiny creatures.

An oystercatcher probes the mud with its stout beak and pulls up a big clam. The clam's shell is hard. But it's no match for the oystercatcher's beak. The bird hammers at the shell until it shatters, then gobbles up the soft body inside.

A Wilson's plover searches for food on the mudflat.

A flock of gulls pecks busily at the mud near a pair of horseshoe crabs.

Gulls cruise overhead on outstretched wings, watching everything that's going on below. They eat crabs and snails—and any scraps that the other birds leave behind.

If accidentally flipped onto its back, a horseshoe crab uses its spiky tail to turn itself over.

The heron spots something moving farther along the mudflat. It's a horseshoe crab. Like a small brown bulldozer, the horseshoe crab plows through the mud, turning up worms and clams. It uses its legs to crush its food and push it into its mouth.

The heron jabs at the horseshoe crab. But its armored shell is hard as a rock. The horseshoe crab suddenly pushes forward, startling the heron. With a harsh croaking call, the big bird flies off to continue its hunt in the estuary.

In some estuaries, millions of horseshoe crabs gather each spring to mate.

A large bed of eelgrass stretches across the estuary like a green meadow.

The heron glides to a landing farther into the estuary. She walks slowly through ankle-deep brackish water. Even at low tide, there is always some water here.

Beds of eelgrass grow on the muddy bottom. Their long, thin leaves sway back and forth like eels as the water moves.

Schools of minnows dart through the eelgrass beds. They hide among the leaves, trying not to be seen by herons, crabs, and other predators. These small fish nibble on eelgrass and feed on plankton.

Seahorses hide in eelgrass beds. These strange-looking fish wrap their tails around the plants to help them stay in one place.

Many kinds of fish begin life in the sheltered waters of the estuary.

21

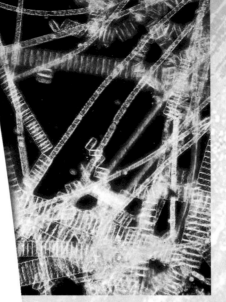

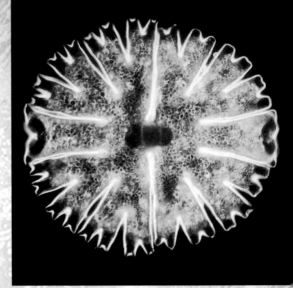

Some animal-like plankton use wiggling, whiplike "tails" to move through the water.

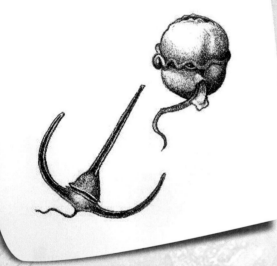

Green plantlike algae thrive in estuary waters. Some grow in long chains of many cells (left). Others are microscopic single cells (right).

Plankton is made up of tiny, free-floating living things. The smallest are just one cell in size. Some types of plankton are plantlike cells called algae. There are algae that look like lacy fans, strings of beads, or tiny boxes with perfectly fitting lids. Other types of plankton are animal-like cells with "tails." Some are shaped like miniature tops—they even spin in the water.

Algae, eelgrass, and other plants that grow in and around the estuary use sunlight to make their own food. They are eaten by many kinds of animals. Plants and algae form the first link in the estuary's food chains.

Low tide has passed. Ocean water is beginning to move into the estuary. Slowly but steadily, the water is getting deeper. In a few hours, it will be high tide.

The heron moves farther up into the estuary, hunting for fish as she goes. She steps carefully around a big patch of oysters. Like clams, oysters have hard shells. They filter plankton from the water for food.

The great blue heron strikes at a passing fish (above). *Bumpy-shelled oysters* (left) *huddle on the bottom.*

Unlike most plants, cordgrass grows well in the brackish water of the estuary. It gets rid of excess salt through tiny structures in its leaves.

Clumps of tall grasses grow near the oyster bed. Smooth cordgrass is the most common grass in this part of the estuary. It has strong stalks and narrow, tough leaves. Other grasses—such as black needlebrush, salt hay grass, three squares, and narrow-leaved cattail—grow here too.

Water winds its way around dense clumps of smooth cordgrass.

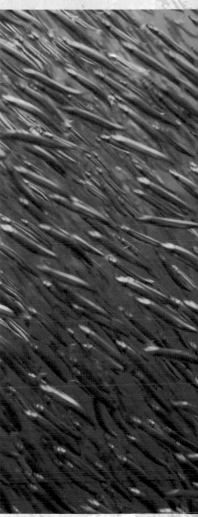

Moving ever so slowly, the heron stalks fish in the shallows (left). In a school of anchovies (below), hundreds of tiny fish swim together as one.

The slender green stems bend and dance in the breeze. They make a whispery, papery sound as they move. All around, insects hum and buzz. Clouds of gnats and mosquitoes hover above the water.

The heron follows the waterways that weave in and around the clumps of grass. A school of anchovies flashes past her legs—too fast for her to strike.

A female blue crab carries her eggs—up to eight million of them—beneath a flap on the underside of her body.

A big blue crab lurks near the base of a tall cordgrass clump. With a massive claw, it reaches out to snare an anchovy that lagged behind the others.

What looks like an empty snail shell lies motionless on the muddy bottom near the blue crab. But when the crab tiptoes off, the shell moves. Long legs poke out of the shell's opening. Then a head appears. It's a hermit crab, making sure the coast is clear. It trundles off across the bottom, dragging along its borrowed home.

Blue crabs eat small fish, worms, clams, and oysters. Large blue crabs will even eat their smaller relatives.

Small anemones and sponges may attach to the shells of hermit crabs. These hitchhikers are natural camouflage that makes the crab harder to see.

Hermit crabs don't have shells of their own. Instead, they use the shells of other animals, especially snails. When a hermit crab outgrows its shell, it searches for a larger one. If the new shell is already occupied, the crab may use its large pincer claws to pull the owner out!

A hermit crab peers out of its borrowed shell.

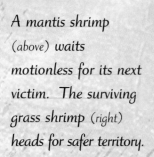

The huge stalked eyes of a mantis shrimp are among the best in the animal world.

The hermit crab disturbs a pair of grass shrimp that are dining on dead grass. They scoot backward in quick spurts to get out of the way.

One grass shrimp swims too close to a predator hiding in the mud. The mantis shrimp slashes out with its large, clawlike arms. It slices the unlucky grass shrimp in half—and settles down to eat.

A mantis shrimp (above) waits motionless for its next victim. The surviving grass shrimp (right) heads for safer territory.

Periwinkles cling to slim grass stems.

The water keeps rising as high tide nears. Periwinkles slowly climb up the slender stalks of grasses to escape hungry crabs and fish. Their spiral shells glint in the sun.

Beneath the climbing snails, a rounded shape breaks the water's surface. A diamondback terrapin peers up at the snails. It stretches out its long neck to reach the nearest one. The terrapin's strong beak cracks the snail's shell open with ease.

A diamondback terrapin's webbed feet help it swim, and its sharp claws give it a good grip in slippery mud.

The diamondback terrapin looks for more food—clams, oysters, or the roots of underwater plants.

After catching three more fish, the heron stops to rest. She fluffs and straightens the feathers on her back and wings with her long beak.

Another fish falls prey to the heron's sharp beak.

A great egret (left) and a snowy egret (below) are both elegantly dressed in pure white feathers.

It's high tide now, and the water is crowded with wading birds hunting for food. A great egret snags a small minnow that struggles—unsuccessfully—to wriggle free. Close by, a reddish egret catches a larger fish that foolishly left its hiding place and wandered into open water.

A reddish egret will often spread its wings to cast a shadow on the water so it can see fish more clearly.

Remarkably long legs allow a reddish egret to wade through fairly deep water.

The marsh wren's nest is attached to reeds well above the water.

A marsh wren sings from a swaying perch.

Other birds are here too. Marsh wrens and seaside sparrows perch on the tips of the grasses, singing as they sway in the wind. The little birds are standing guard over their nests. The nests are woven out of soft blades of grass. They shelter spotted eggs that are ready to hatch.

Kek-kek-kek-kek-kek. From somewhere in the grass comes the rattling call of the clapper rail. A secretive bird, it builds its nest in a clump of cordgrass and hunts for fiddler crabs and snails.

Hidden in the thick grass, a clapper rail (above) is hard to spot. Another rail (left) leaves its hiding place to search for a meal.

Standing in the water beside the grass clumps, the heron has finished smoothing her feathers. She is ready to fly. She takes off, skimming over the grasses and then soaring higher and higher into the sky.

Beneath her, the estuary looks much different than it did just a few hours ago. The mudflats are completely covered by water. The brackish water in the eelgrass beds is deeper too. At high tide, the estuary is full of water.

A pair of cormorants bobs on the water. First one, then the other, tucks its head and dives.

The heron flies across the estuary (above). *Bubbles stream behind a cormorant as it dives* (right).

The cormorants are chasing a spotted sea trout. Dark gray above and silvery below, the big fish streaks toward the bottom. It is too fast for the cormorants and disappears into the depths.

The cormorants head back to the surface. But on their way up, one spots a slow-moving catfish. The bird kicks hard with its webbed feet and snares the fish in its hooked bill.

The cormorant surfaces with a prize.

Cow-nosed rays occasionally swim into the estuary from the ocean, looking for clams and oysters to eat.

Stinging tentacles trail gracefully behind the bowl-shaped body of a jellyfish.

These deeper waters of the estuary are full of life. A jellyfish, ghostly and pale, drifts past. It snags plankton to eat with its long tentacles. It has been carried into the estuary from the ocean with the tide. Another visitor from the sea—a young cow-nosed ray—glides through the water like a fleeting shadow.

A school of menhaden cruises near the surface, attracting a flock of gulls. Many feet below, a black drum feeds near the bottom. It plucks a snail from the mud and swallows it whole. Menhaden and drum swim into the estuary from the ocean. They may stay for many weeks, feasting on smaller animals that live in the estuary's quiet waters.

Many ocean fish also come to lay their eggs. The eggs are swept far up into the estuary by the incoming tide. The young fish that hatch from the eggs stay in shallow areas for many months, eating and growing. The quiet waters of the estuary are like a huge nursery, a relatively safe place for small fish to live until they are big enough to survive in the open ocean.

A large black drum (top) prowls through deep water. Young striped bass (above) won't leave the estuary until they are large enough to survive the perils of the sea.

When the heron's chicks first hatched, they were little more than clumps of fuzzy down.

The heron reaches the far end of the estuary, near the mouth of the river. Shrubs and trees grow along the riverbank. The bird lands on the edge of her nest near the top of a small black gum tree. Her three chicks chirp out a greeting.

The heron brings up the fish she has recently eaten and feeds them to her chicks. When they have eaten, it is time to rest for a while in the late afternoon sun.

The large, flat nest of a great blue heron is made of twigs and branches woven tightly together.

Three hungry heron chicks beg for food from their mother.

A raccoon family hunts for food in the shallow water.

As shadows lengthen in the estuary, a black-masked raccoon and her baby trot past below the heron's nest. They have spent the day sleeping in a hollow log. Now they are hurrying down to the shallow waters around the edge of the estuary. They will hunt for crabs and shrimps and clams.

The heron watches the raccoons disappear into the shadows. Moments later, four young foxes appear. They are following the raccoons. The foxes sniff the air. Then they move on toward the water, slipping away on softly padded paws.

Young foxes rest at the water's edge before the start of their evening hunt.

The sun sets over the estuary as the tide begins to go out.

In the estuary, the water is beginning to drain away from the land again. Out on the mudflat, patches of muddy bottom appear. Clams and oysters close their shells. Worms pull down deep into their burrows. Soon it will be low tide again.

From her nest, the heron looks out over the estuary. Day is giving way to night. The colors of the setting sun glow in the still water.

Life in the estuary revolves around the changing tide and the changing seasons. In a few weeks, the heron's chicks will be old enough to start feeding on their own. They will wade through the brackish water. They will learn to catch fish. And they will learn the rhythm of the estuary, their home between a river and the sea.

As night falls, the heron chicks settle down to sleep. In the coming days, they'll leave the nest and learn to hunt in the estuary on their own.

for further
Information
about the Estuary

Books

Aiken, Zora. *Finding Birds in the Chesapeake Marsh: A Child's First Look.* Centreville, MD: Tidewater Publishing, 2001.

Arnosky, Jim. *Following the Coast.* New York: HarperCollins, 2004.

Collard, Sneed B., III. *Our Wet World.* Watertown, MA: Charlesbridge Publishing, 1998.

Dunlap, Julie. *Extraordinary Horseshoe Crabs.* Minneapolis: Carolrhoda Books, 1999.

Fleisher, Paul. *Salt Marsh.* Tarrytown, NY: Marshall Cavendish, 1999.

Gibbons, Gail. *Marshes and Swamps.* New York: Holiday House, 1998.

Jewett, Sarah Orne. *A White Heron: A Story of Maine.* New York: T. Y. Crowell, 1963.

Ketchum, Mary O'Neill. *Clapper Rail: The Secret Bird of the Marsh.* New York: Henry Holt & Company, 1997.

Lewin, Ted. *When the Rivers Go Home.* New York: Atheneum, 1992.

Miller, Sara Swan. *Wading Birds: From Herons to Hammerkops.* New York: Franklin Watts, 2001.

Pringle, Laurence. *Estuaries: Where Rivers Meet the Sea.* New York: MacMillan, 1973.

Staub, Frank. *Herons.* Minneapolis: Lerner Publications, 1997.

Walker, Sally M. *Life in an Estuary.* Minneapolis, Lerner Publications, 2003.

———. *Sea Horses.* Minneapolis: Carolrhoda Books, 1999.

Websites

Chesapeake Bay Program < http://www.chesapeakebay.net/ >

This website is all about the Chesapeake Bay, the largest estuary in the United States.

U.S. Environmental Protection Agency—
National Estuary Program
< http://www.epa.gov/owow/estuaries/ >

This government agency website shows what the U.S. government is doing to protect estuaries around the country.

Tampa Bay Estuary Program
< http://www.tbep.org/ >

This website shows a large, human-populated estuary—how the ecosystem and the cities coexist and how people have brought a polluted estuary back to health.

The Oregon Estuary Plan Book
< http://www.inforain.org/mapsatwork /oregonestuary/ >

This website is all about estuaries in Oregon on the Pacific coast.

Photo Acknowledgments

The photographs in this book are used with the permission of: Visuals Unlimited (© Sol Levine, p. 4; © Martin Miller, p. 6; © Marc Epstein, p. 7 (bottom); © Bernd Wittich, p. 10 (top and bottom); © David Wrobel, p. 12; © Charles McRae, pp. 13, 24; © Jim Merli, p. 16; © Rob & Ann Simpson, pp. 17, 18, 23 (bottom), 30; © John D. Cunningham, pp. 19, 26; © Michael DeMocker, p. 20; © David M. Phillips, p. 22 (left); © Mike Abbey, p. 22 (right); © R. DeGoursey, p. 27; © Marty Snyderman, p.28 (top); © David Addison, p. 28 (bottom); © Charles Melton, p. 34; © D. Wrobel, p. 38; © Paul A. Grecian, p. 44; © Gustav Verderber, p. 45); © Thomas Mark Szelog, pp. 7 (top), 25 (left), 31, 36 (top); © James P. Rowan, pp. 8 (top and bottom); © Heather R. Davidson, pp. 9, 23 (top), 32 (left and right); Tom Stack & Associates (© Ken W. Davis, p. 11; © Joe McDonald, p. 33); © HNPA/Bill Coster, p. 14; © Roger Archibald, p. 15; © Robert Noonan, pp. 21, 39 (right); © Michael Aw/Lonely Planet Images, p. 25; Bruce Coleman Inc. (© George H. Harrison, p. 29; © John Shaw, p. 41); © Joe McDonald, pp. 35 (top), 37; © Doug Wechsler/ VIREO, p. 35 (bottom); © Henry Ausloos/ Animalsanimals, p. 36 (bottom); © David Liebman, p. 39 (left); © Richard P. Smith, p. 40; PhotoDisc Royalty Free by Getty Images, p. 42; © Brian Kenney, p. 43.

Cover photographs by © Ryan C. Taylor/Tom Stack and Associates (background) and © Thomas Mark Szelog (heron).

Index

Numbers in **bold** refer to photos and drawings.